Summary

of

The Great Revolt
Salena Zito & Brad Todd

Conversation Starters

By BookHabits

Bonus Downloads
Get Free Books with ___Any Purchase___ *of* Conversation Starters!

Every purchase comes with a FREE download!

Add spice to any conversation
Never run out of things to say
Spend time with those you love

Get it Now

or Click Here.

Scan Your Phone

Tips for Using Conversation Starters:

EVERY GOOD BOOK CONTAINS A WORLD FAR DEEPER THAN the surface of its pages. Questions herein are designed to bring us beneath the surface of the page and invite us into the world that lives on. These questions can be used to:

- Foster a deeper understanding of the book
- Promote an atmosphere of discussion for groups
- Assist in the study of the book, either individually or corporately
- Explore unseen realms of the book as never seen before

Table of Contents

Introducing *The Great Revolt*

*T*HE GREAT REVOLT IS A BOOK THAT TAKES A closer look at the people who voted for Donald Trump, presents their real life circumstances and personal views on election issues and reasons why they voted for their president. Written by first-time authors Salena Zito and Brad Todd, it is cited for its empathetic approach that political scholars nor politicians have not thought of doing.

Zito and Todd traveled to ten swing counties to interview 300 Trump voters to get to know them better. They discovered that they are the voters who have been hiding in plain sight, unseen and unrecognized by the media, the political parties, and the election scholars. Their presence was finally felt when they united their votes in 2016, causing the greatest upset in the history of American elections. The authors hail from these Midwestern swing states and are knowledgeable of the culture and are therefore capable of presenting a closer view of the voters who were branded by media as angry, racist, male, and rural. They present a different side of the voters and conclude that they cannot be limited to any particular category in education level, income bracket, or party allegiance. Instead, what unites them according to the authors is their preference for pragmatism over ideology, focus on the local over the global, and their demand for respect from America's leaders. After presenting a real life view of these voters and their personal and political motivations, the authors ask the question-- what comes next after the swing voters phenomenon and the resulting shake-up of the American political system?

The authors start the book by discussing how voters like Bonnie Smith are hidden in plain sight and give a socio-economic profile of a swing county like Ashtabula where Smith resides. They stress that the unexpected upset in the recent elections should not come as a surprise. They likened the elections to that of consumer behavior which is open and changing in a dynamic market. The authors explain their choice of counties which include farm areas in Iowa and Wisconsin, formerly bustling industrial centers in Lake Erie and Mississippi, and Detroit suburbs. They explain the methods they employed in doing their research, carrying out face-to-face interviews with people in diners, coffee shops, watering holes, bed-and-breakfasts, places where locals gather as a community. They avoided interstates and chain restaurants as a result.

To support their interviews, Zito and Todd did empirical data analysis and the survey research they called The Great Revolt Survey which was fielded to 2,000 Trump voters equally divided among Wisconsin, Iowa, Michigan, Pennsylvania, and Ohio counties.

The book outlines seven archetypes of Trump voters, with each category featuring interviews of voters who represent the archetypes of swing voters. The swing voters are variously described as blue collar workers, churchgoers, and "silent suburban moms." Many of them had incomes under $75,000. The interviews are cited by critics as deeply sensitive, showing empathy for the people and their concerns. The authors focus on uncovering the personal concerns, religious faith, and economic challenges that the voters face. The concerns that resonated most with them include the restoration manufacturing jobs, protection and access to Medicare and social security, and the appointment of conservative supreme court judges.

Some critics cited that the racism issue that was raised against Trump voters was given minimal coverage and therefore not fully explored and explained in the book. Their views on the immigrant issue and the wall between Mexico were not elaborated on as well. The voters expressed disillusionment with the Democrats and Barack Obama for allowing globalism to take over their towns. Their pro-life values and conservative beliefs were mocked which gave them enough reason to vote for someone who vowed to protect their faith from desecration even if he does not share their moral values, at least as far as the sanctity of marriage and monogamy is concerned. The authors also highlighted the feeling of deep connection the voters have with Trump, seeing him as the man who dared mock traditional political beliefs and being a man of his own person. The authors expressed interest in the staying power of this coalition between populists and conservatives and its influence in future elections. Though they do not provide answers to the question of what comes next after the unlikely coalition, critics believe that they contributed to the political discussion by reporting on an aspect that political scholars and the traditional politicians failed to tap into.

The Great Revolt was highly praised by Trump himself who tweeted about the book, recommending it to his followers. Critics cite the authors' deep empathy for the misunderstood voters and convincingly conveyed this in the book.

Discussion Questions

"Get Ready to Enter a New World"

Tip: Begin with questions dealing with broader issues to ensure ample time for quality discussions. Read through all discussion questions before engaging.

~~~

question 1

To interview people for the book, the authors looked for Trump voters in farm counties, suburbs, fading industrial centers, in diners, watering holes, bed-and-breakfasts, and coffee shops. Why this particular places and not interstates and chain restaurants?

~~~

~~~

question 2

The authors used empirical data analysis and the Great Revolt Survey which was done among 2,000 Trump voters. How do these help the book's credibility among readers? How does it make you feel that the book is based on these research?

~~~

~~~

question 3

The authors speak of hidden in plain sight voters who were least expected to vote for Trump. Who are these voters? Why are they hidden in plain sight?

~~~

~~~

question 4

The authors believe that they have to understand these hidden in plain sight voters. They want to know their angsts and aspirations. Why? What result do they want to get from their interviews?

~~~

~~~

question 5

Bonnie Smith of Ashtabula County, Ohio always voted Democrat in the past elections. In the 2016 elections however, she decided to vote for Trump. What was her reason for her change of mind?

~~~

~~~

question 6

The book mentions the issue of gun use as a motivating factor for Trump's supporters. What are the authors' stand on gun use?

~~~

~~~

question 7

Trump's supporters are described by the authors as blue-collar workers, churchgoers, and suburban moms. How do the authors explain the relation between economic income and the voters' decision to vote for Trump?

~~~

~~~

question 8

According to the authors' interviews, Trumps supporters wanted R-E-S-P-E-C-T. Why do they not feel respected by the democrats?

~~~

~~~

question 9

Trump supporters voted for him for particular social and economic issues they want addressed. What are these?

~~~

question 10

The authors stressed the personal connection that Trump has with his supporters, something that Hillary Clinton was not able to do. What do the voters say that reflect their connection with Trump?

~~~

question 11

The authors categorize Trump supporters into seven sub-groups. Which of the groups is particularly striking to you? Why?

~~~

question 12

The book cites that well-educated people voted for Trump in Ashtabula county. What is the reason for this? In contrast, what reason did the authors give for well-educated people not wanting to vote for Trump?

~ ~ ~

question 13

The book cites interviewees who claim they are not racist, contrary to the claim that Trump supporters are racist. What do they say about their not being racist? Are you satisfied or enlightened about their racial views?

~ ~ ~

~~~

question 14

The book features Jill Gilmore who voted for Trump despite her belief that he is not a morally upstanding man. What were her reasons for voting for him? Why is it okay for her to vote for someone who is not representative of her morals and ethics?

~~~

~~~

question 15

The book discusses Trump's use of Twitter as an important element in his winning the elections. How did Twitter become a factor in his victory?

~~~

~~~

question 16

The *Washington Examiner* says it is the authors'
empathy for the misunderstood voters that was
conveyed in the book. Did you feel for the voters
who were interviewed? Why? Why not?

~~~

~ ~ ~

question 17

The Guardian review says the the authors "convincingly capture the anger and angst" that caused voters to turn to Trump. How do you feel about the anger and the angst that moved voters to veer towards Trump?

~ ~ ~

~ ~ ~

question 18

Trump tweeted praises for the book. Will you recommend the book to others because he endorsed it? Why? Why not?

~ ~ ~

~ ~ ~

question 19

USA Today says the book researched on material that is useful for both Democrats and Republicans, and that they should "study and internalize" it. How will the book be of importance to Democrats and Republicans?

~ ~ ~

~~~

question 20

The *Pittsburgh Post-Gazette* questions the authors' argument that "social pressure that comes with living exclusively among other college graduates" caused educated voters to vote against Trump. Why do you think the reviewer does not agree with the authors on this? Do you find the authors' argument well-supported?

~~~

Introducing the Author

SALENA ZITO IS A REPORTER, COLUMNIST, and a CNN contributor. As a journalist who has reported on political events for the past two decades, she has interviewed all past presidents since Gerald Ford, and all vice presidents since Walter Mondale. A native of Pittsburgh, Pennsylvania, she held various occupations before turning to journalism. She was owner of a pie business and a theater which staged Reservoir Dogs, and worked for the Pittsburgh Steelers.

Zito prefers to travel by road rather than by air. In this way, she gets to see the towns and communities where many Americans live, and is acquainted with their lives up close. She gets to understand how politics and national policies influence the lives of common people. With her 14 year old Jeep Liberty, she has covered three swing midterm elections and three presidential cycles in the past decade. She calls herself a history geek and has kept herself well-informed by visiting the history archives of the Gettysburg, Harpers Ferry, Antietam, and the Indian War National Parks in Fort Necessity and Jumonville Glen. Zito is also passionate about cycling, having covered around 2,000 trail miles a year. She completed a solo ride traversing West Newton Pennsylvania and

Washington D.C. She spends every Sunday with her immediate and extended family.

Brad Todd is known for his expertise in making ads for members of the Republican Party. However, he admits that he was among those who predicted that Trump's candidacy in the Republican party's primaries will not move forward. He lead the group of consultants for the House takeover executed by the Republicans in 2010. With his company OnMessage Inc., Todd was responsible for creating ads for Ron Johnson, and Rick Scott who won the governorship of Florida. He and his firm also made ads that resulted to the defeat of 11 Democrats in Congress. Other significant clients include Bobby Jindal who won the first Indian-American position for Governor in America, and Senator Scott Brown who had an unexpected win in Massachusetts. Critics in traditional print media praised Todd's previous work for politicians, calling it "devastatingly effective" and was cited among the ten best campaigns in the 2010.

Todd has worked with the National Rifle Association and sports teams, providing strategy and branding advice for these groups. He is founder of Coach to Cure MD which helped raise money for research on Duchenne Muscular Dystrophy.

Todd co-founded On Message Inc. With Curt Anderson and Wes Anderson. Before this, he was worked with the Todd & Castellanos Creative Group. He was one of the firm's partners.

Todd is the holder of a Master's degree from Missouri University's School of Journalism. His family have been residents of Roane County, East Tennessee for five generations now. He currently lives in Old Town Alexandria, Virginia with his wife and two children.

Zito and Todd argue in their book that well-educated people vote for Democrats if they belong to communities that show wide disparity in community members' educational levels. They believe that it is social pressure that highly influences their political choices.

Bonus Downloads

*Get Free Books with **Any Purchase** of* Conversation Starters!

Every purchase comes with a FREE download!

Add spice to any conversation
Never run out of things to say
Spend time with those you love

Get it Now

or Click Here.

Scan Your Phone

Fireside Questions

"What would you do?"

Tip: These questions can be a fun exercise as it spurs creativity among the readers by allowing alternate scene endings and "if this was you" questions.

~~~

question 21

Salena Zito held various occupations before turning to journalism. She was owner of a pie business and a theater which staged Reservoir Dogs, and worked for the Pittsburgh Steelers. How has her work experience helped her journalism career and in the writing of this book?

~~~

~~~

question 22

Zito prefers to travel by road rather than by air.
Why?

~~~

~~~

question 23

She calls herself a history geek and has kept herself well-informed by visiting the history archives. How has knowledge of history helped her as a writer?

~~~

question 24

Brad Todd admits that he was among those who predicted that Trump's candidacy in the Republican party's primaries will not move forward. How has this affected his work as a political strategist?

~ ~ ~

question 25

Todd was responsible for creating ads for Republicans who were successfully elected. Can you name these politicians? How important were Todd's ads in their success?

~ ~ ~

~~~

question 26

The authors start the book by discussing how voters like Bonnie Smith are hidden in plain sight. If you are the author, how would you want to start the book? What story or data would you present first?

~~~

~ ~ ~

question 27

The authors likened the elections to that of consumer behavior which is open and changing in a dynamic market. If you are the author, to what will you compare the elections to? Why?

~ ~ ~

question 28

The book outlines seven archetypes of Trump voters. If you are to give subtitles or names for these archetypes, what titles would you give?

~~~

question 29

Some critics cited that the racism issue that was raised against Trump voters was given minimal coverage and therefore not fully explored and explained in the book. If you are the author, how would you tackle the issue of racism among the Trump voters?

~~~

~~~

question 30

The authors ask but do not answer the question--
what comes next after the swing voters
phenomenon and the resulting shake-up of the
American political system? If you are to write a
sequel to this book, what would you focus on?
Why?

~~~

Quiz Questions

"Ready to Announce the Winners?"

Tip: Create a leaderboard and track scores to see who gets the most correct answers. Winners required. Prizes optional.

~~~

quiz question 1

The authors start the book by discussing how voters like Bonnie Smith are hidden in plain sight and give a socio-economic profile of a swing county like _____ where Smith resides.

~~~

~~~

quiz question 2

Zito and Todd did empirical data analysis and the survey research they called _____.

~~~

~~~

quiz question 3

The_____ voters are variously described as blue collar workers, churchgoers, and "silent suburban moms," among others.

~~~

~~~

quiz question 4

True or False: The book outlines ten archetypes of Trump voters, with each category featuring interviews of voters who represent the archetypes of swing voters.

~~~

~~~

quiz question 5

True or False: The authors focus on uncovering the personal concerns, religious faith, and economic challenges that the voters face.

~~~

~ ~ ~

quiz question 6

True or False: The voters expressed disillusionment with the Democrats and Barack Obama for allowing globalism to take over their towns.

~ ~ ~

~~~

quiz question 7

True or False: The book contributed to the political discussion by reporting on an aspect that political scholars and the traditional politicians failed to tap into.

~~~

~~~

quiz question 8

Salena Zito is a native of _____

~~~

quiz question 9

True or False: She has covered three swing midterm elections and three presidential cycles in the past decade.

~~~

quiz question 10

True or False: She spends every Sunday with her friends and co-workers.

~~~

~ ~ ~

quiz question 11

Brad Todd has worked with the _____, providing strategy and branding advice for this Association.

~ ~ ~

~~~

quiz question 12

True or False: Todd is founder of Coach to Cure MD which helped raise money for research on Duchenne Muscular Dystrophy.

~~~

Quiz Answers

1. Ashtabula
2. The Great Revolt Survey
3. swing
4. False
5. True
6. True
7. True
8. Pittsburgh, Pennsylvania
9. True
10. False
11. National Rifle Association
12. True

Ways to Continue Your Reading

E VERY month, our team runs through a wide selection of books to pick the best titles for readers and reading groups, and promotes these titles to our thousands of readers – sometimes with free downloads, sale dates, and additional brochures.

Click here to sign up for these benefits.

If you have not yet read the original work or would like to read it again, you can purchase the original book here.

Bonus Downloads
Get Free Books with *Any Purchase* of Conversation Starters!

Every purchase comes with a FREE download!

Add spice to any conversation
Never run out of things to say
Spend time with those you love

Get it Now

or Click Here.

Scan Your Phone

On the Next Page...

If you found this book helpful to your discussions and rate it a 4 or 5, please write us a review on the next page.

Any length would be fine but we'd appreciate hearing you more! We'd be very encouraged.

Till next time,

BookHabits

"Loving Books is Actually a Habit"